# Still I Stayed
## I'M ALIVE

Nagamalli Manasvi

## Still I Stayed

Copyright © 2025 Nagamalli Manasvi

All rights reserved. No part of this book may be reproduced, stored in a retrieval system, or transmitted in any form or by any means, electronic, mechanical, photocopying, recording, or otherwise, without the prior written permission of the author.

This book is sold as is, without any warranties, express or implied. The author and publisher are not responsible for any problems that may arise from using this book. If you have a problem with the book, your only option is to return it for a refund. The author agrees to protect the publisher from any legal issues that may arise from the book's content. Any legal disputes about this book will be handled according to the laws of the constitution of India

Publisher: Inkscribe Media Pvt. Ltd

ISBN Number: 978-1-966421-54-2

Welcome, dear reader. And thank you for making the decision to read this book. That decision indicates that you have an interest in changing your life for the better. It shows that you want to learn something new that will help you improve your present situation.

You've made a good decision, for the simple decision to learn something new is one of the first steps in personal and professional growth. Learning is critical to staying mentally and physically sharp no matter what your age. It's been said that when you stop learning, you begin to die. So don't ever stop learning!

There is magic in this book. Not so much in the words but in the results that will happen for you as you go through the processes that may fit your situation best. You'll discover how to make your dreams and desires become reality. You'll find ways to become the person you want to be. You'll learn to find happiness and satisfaction in accomplishing your goals.

Are you truly happy in your current relationships with yourself, your significant other, your career, your community, your constituency or any other people or things with whom you interact? If not, there is only one person who can change things to make you truly happy. And that person is YOU!

And I'm thankfully to my parents who supports me to doing this…

~HOPE YOU WILL LIKE BOOK…THANK YOU

# Introduction

There comes a time in life when everything we once believed to be permanent begins to fall apart — friendships grow distant, love turns cold, and the people we thought would always stay begin to disappear without a reason. It's in these moments, when we feel the most alone, that we are quietly rebuilding ourselves.

This is the story of someone who once had nothing but broken bonds — a person who lost friends not through fights, but through silence, time, and change. Someone whose family, once scattered and shaken, slowly began to rely on them — the quiet one, the forgotten one, the one who never gave up. They rose, not out of pride, but out of necessity, becoming the backbone of a family that once didn't see their worth.

But this isn't just about rising. It's about understanding that love — true love — begins from within. Self- love isn't a trend; it's a foundation. It's waking up and choosing yourself on days when no one else does. It's holding your own hand through the chaos and reminding your heart that it is still enough. Even when emotions overwhelm us, even when we break — healing starts by allowing ourselves to feel, not fear.

We also learn, sometimes painfully, that not all love is pure. There are those who pretend, who stay for their own gain, and those who leave when you need them the most. But that doesn't make your love any less real — it only makes your heart more valuable.

In a world that never stops rushing, we often forget the power of "now. " The present moment is all we truly own. Learning to live here — not in the past we wish we could fix, or the future we fear — is the first step to peace. And while we care for others, we must not forget to care for our health, our body, our mind — for they carry us through everything.

This book is a reminder. Of growth after loss. Of strength in silence. Of the quiet kind of love that begins with you

# Contents

*Introduction*.................................................................................... 5

Becoming my own Home ............................................................ 9

When Friendship Fades ............................................................. 15

The Value of now… .................................................................. 20

Value Before they leave! ........................................................... 28

Importance of Being Present ..................................................... 34

The Art of Laziness ................................................................... 37

The Silent Distance ................................................................... 40

Left Behide ................................................................................ 44

The Strong One ........................................................................ 48

Life is Like a Cinema ................................................................ 52

People Leaving Without Warning ............................................. 54

The Becominggg… ................................................................... 58

Literally show me a healthy person' ......................................... 60

The Girl Who Gave Everything…. ........................................... 65

*Final Note* .................................................................................. 69

*The Ones Who Stayed When No One Else Did!* ....................... 72

*Two Silences, One Heart"* ......................................................... 79

# Chapter 1

# Becoming my own Home

Start with Self-Love…

Imagine. We are in the moment of everything brokes us. There is one to heal us.

There was a time I kept waiting for Someone to come and fix me. I believed, healing would come from a friend who cared enough. From a family that suddenly understood me or from Love that felt like magic I waited - far Someone to see me to hear the part of me that were breaking, to save me from myself.

But "No one Came.

And that Silence? It was the beginning of everything.

No one teaches you how to be alone. we grow op Surrounded by the idea that happiness is found in others - In Being chosen. So, when people (or) grow distant when Love turns cold or One-Sided It' Start to feel like you're the promble Like you're not enough And for a while I belived that too.

It was About Loving myself. first.

That's when it begins - The journery of myself

Far the longest time I thought harde was a A feeling someone else could give me belived If I just loved harder gave more, Stayed loyal - Someone would finally choose me in the way was choosing them But the truth you can give your whale heart to Someone and they can still Leave you can be the best Version of yourself.

Still won't be enough far the worng people. The truth Shattered me But it also saved me

Self-Love isn't just affirmations or Skincare routines. It's doing the hard thing. It's walking away from what hurts. even when you're still in the love with the idea of it. It's learning to be okay with your own company - to sit with Silence and not feel alone in it. It's holding your own hand when no one else does.

The day I stopped waiting for someone to come Save me I saved myself.

Its realizing that your loneliness doesn't mean Youre unlovable. It means your growing…

shedding old versions of yourself and Learning to Live within…ITS NOT SELFISH TO LOVE YOURSELF

ITS, NECESSARY

Because,

people will Leave. Even the ones you thought Never would Circumstance changes.

Love can fade Friends can grow apart. And through all of that - youre the only constant in your Life.

So why Not be your own safe place?

Let your mind to kind to you. Let your heart forgive you. Let your body can feel rest - Not Just Surival when you make peace with yourself you stop begging for it form other& And that?

That's real freedom.

You don't Need to be perfect to be whole. You Just Need to be honest with yourself. About what hurts? what you deserve what you've been through and where you to want to go from here.

Every Time you choose to stay

...

And I promise you

-Your becoming your Home.

IT'S THE MOST BEAUTIFULL PLACE...

ITS rewriting every lie your belived in yourself That you're too emotional. To Sensitive To much. lot enough Self Love Says: you always were

## Still I Stayed

The one day I'd meet someone who would understand every part of me without needing explation. That the Right person would notice the sadness behide my smile…

That Someone anyone- stay long enough.

But the day Never came. At least, Not the way I expected…

what came instead were people who left, without closure. Friends who grew distant.

Consversations that faded into silence - Days where I questioned if I was hard to Love. If I was doing too much If I was not enough. I gave everything I had thinking that If I just kept giving Someone would finally choose me the way

I was choosing them,

But all that giving the empty.

For a long time!

I tried my worth to how others Save me If Someone Loved me, I felt Valuable If they Left. I felt Broken my confidence was like a mirror- Reflecting only what Others gaves me But mirrors Can shatter AND,

One day. when mine did I had to start picking up the pieces alone

That was the first time I Asked myself! what If I Loved myself

> without permisson?

- without waiting?
- without Conditions?

And the Answer changed Everything;

Self-Love is Not Loud. It is Not always visible Sometimes it's Just choosing to get out of bed when your heart is heavy. Sometimes its forgiving yourself for years of self-blame.

Your Learn to set boundaries Not to push People away But to protect the version of you that's finally healing. you stop chasing the ones who treat your presence like an option you Let go Not because Stopped caring but because you strated Caring about yourself a little more.

The day you choose to Love yourself.

And I hope you Never Leave.

# DAY 1

MAYBE WE WILL NEVER MEET

BUT…

WE CAN STILL WALK TOGETHER LIKE TO INFINITY AND BEYOND…

# Chapter 2

# When Friendship Fades

In this generation - Friendships starts quickly and fade even faster….

**Friendship** in this Generation Needs to be redefined It's Not about who replies fast OR posts on you on stories. It's about who checks on you when you go Quiet. who Listens, really Listens who celebrates your growth without competing, who stays even when it's inconvenient. That's rare. And it's real.

So yes-Losing friend's hurts. It changes but it also clear space for people who are aligned with the Version of you that's Becoming. The ones who match your energy. your heart, your Values.

We Bond over late - Night texts, Shared playlists, inside Jokes and "I feel like I've known you forever" Conversations. One moments your telling them everything your fears, your dreams, your worst days-and it feels like you've found your person your safe space

And Then, One day It shifts,

Not Because of a fight Not because of the Something you said "But because life moved forward and four some reason they didn't take you with them…

At first It subtle…The messages slow down The laughs get shorter the energy feels different you keep reaching out They pulling back you tell your self they're Busy Just tried. Just distracted…

But deep down…Something in you knowns The friendship is fading.

This generation fast bonds but doesn't talk about the emotional responsibility. Everyone wants connections - few want connect commitment. It's easy to get close to someone It takes, real efforts to stay close. we're to used to replacing people when they don't" Vibe" with us anymore...

But Some friendships deserved more than that,

The truth is people change you will too. The version of you that connected with them may No longer exist. You may heal grow (or) Outgrow And while that can feel like a loss. It's also a sign of becoming.

You're not wrong for missing them, you're not weak for feeling it deeply - Missing Someone who was once.... Your whole world is human is such is true relation.

**If they didn't maintain that Then you're Such a pure Soul**

**THE WEIGHT OF ONE:SIDE FRIENSHIPS**

I was always the one who cared more...

I Remembered every detail like their favorites, and the little things they said to me in passing that no one else noticed

I was checked in when they disappeared who stayed up late listening to their rants who kept, slowing up even when I felt like I was going slowly fading in their world

whenever their phone lit up. I hoped it was me they were texting back. But most of the days. I was left on Seen (or) worse-forgotten.

I told myself they were just busy. That maybe they didn't realize how distant they had become. I excused the missed calls, the dry replies the times they didn't Show up when I Needed them the most.

But deep down. I knew. I was holding into a connection, they had already for both of us.

One-sided friendships is like clapping with one-hand you keep trying to make a sound but no matter how hard You tryy. It only leaves you tired and sore.

letting go wasn't easy. I grieved a friendship that Never fully existed the way I Imaged it.

**Space for real peoples…**

**Space for Peace…**

**Space for me…**

> ➢ They'll show up-just like you do.

**Some friendship don't end with big fights**

They end with a slow fade-out like messages daft on Seen calls Never returned and promises that quietly disappeared And that silence? It can be doubts than any argument…

And it hurts in a different way - because You weren't ready to let go!

You kept showing up. you kept remembering the Little things you still wanted to share your wins your heartbreaks. Your random thoughts But they stopped Showing interest And Over time you Stopped trying too.

**That's how most friendships End Today!"**

> ➢ Not with a goodbye. but with both people Slowly pretending it doesn't hurt.

But you known what's brave?

Choosing Not to hold on to one-sided effort Choosing to stop watering a connection that doesn't grow,

> **choosing yourself.**

**"Final Section of Celebrating True friendship"**

Not All friendships Paid Some grow with you through the versions of yourself even you don't recognize....

A real friend doesn't need daily texts to prove their Love They just know you could go weeks without talking and when you finally call - Nothing a changed No awkward. No keeping Scores Just Understanding Just presence.

> They don't flinch when you show your broken pieces
> They don't leave when you cancel plans for the third time because your mental health isn't okay...
> They check in when you're quiet

Sometimes All your really Need in this Life is one person who feels like

**All you Need only One"**

That's the kind of friendships that doesn't need daily proof

-just genuine love

Because even one true friend.... is a lifetime gift And After reading this Say to thanks to your one person who stays, who fights for you. who always loves you.

**I'm the one feels every line Own.**

# Day 2

BECAUSE I CARRY IT WELL...

DOESN'T MEAN ITS NOT HEAVY...

# Chapter 3

# The Value of now…

We live in a world where everything looks. Perfect, but almost nothing feels Real Relationships have become status friendship have become competition.

And Love? Love is now a word people use too quickly and mean too little.

People don't connect they compare. They don't Stay they get bored: They don't listen, they wait to reply.

And in all this fake loud glittering Noise - The people who are real get drowned out.

**We trust too fast**

**we expect too much.**

**we fall for people who show, us attention Not intention We fall in Love with the ideas of someone –Not the reality.**

And in the process. We forgot ourselves. We give everything expecting in the same return. And we break when it doesn't come back.

Even though we're already losing ourselves by keeping efforts on them.

> ➤ **This is the cost of forgetting the Value of now…**

**And Along Ago**

- ➤ Right Now Someone is smiling in public and breaking in Silence.
- ➤ Right Now, Someone is trying their best but still feeling like it's not enough.

We wake up and the first thing we do is reach. For Our phones - Not our peace. Before we step into the day. Our minds are already filled with someone else's Life.

Someone else's success, someone else's filtered highlight reel. We're chasing versions of ourselves that only exists for the world's approval not our Own in that constant race, we forget to Ask: **Am I even happy with who I am?**

College is supposed to be the time we discover ourselves but often it's the place we start to dose ourselves we're balancing classes. expectations emotional baggage and comparison - All while Pretending we're doing fire. The truth is many Students are mentally drowning while academically passing you sit in classroom feeling invisible. You walk through hallways smiling, while your mind is full of Noise you can't explain to anyone.

No one see the pressure that builds up inside. When you're trying to be everything and everyone.

**All of that you forget to Just be you!**

Then there are the peoples Friends who once felt like home start feeling like Strangers realize Some only Stayed for the good parts.

Some friendships aren't lost to arguments they lost to Silence, inconsistency, and distance. The worst

kind of heartbreaks isn't from relationships It's from the people who said they'd always be there and then quietly weren't Fake people don't Just exist on instagram - they just exist beside us behind smiles. And it hurts deeply to realize that the love you gave, So freely was taken for granted. taken

Even the closest people - family partners, best friend -can feel distant we dive in generation where people talk more, but connect less where everyone is available. But No one is really present. Conversations feel rushed Emotions get ignored Everyone is Busy - but with what! In the Gush of growing up we forget to Check in. with Ourselves.

**The Value of Now.**

We keep postponing peace.

we think I'll feel better once I get that Job. once I leave this college

Once I meet the Right person.

But peace isn't something you find later

It's something you create. Now!

That's what this Generation has mastered-silent Suffering and the Scariest post is that it's become Normal.

- ➢ We don't talk about the Nights we over think everything
- ➢ We don't talk about how sometimes, even good days feel empty.
- ➢ We don't talk about the guilt of being tried when you should be grateful".
- ➢ We don't talk about how it hurts you when people don't check on you like you do four them.

But if you're reading this and relating to even one of those things.

"you're Not Alone"

Because Now- this every moment – matters

**The present moment!**

With all mess, Pain and beauty - is your teacher. It's showing you who's real who're temporary what you Need and what you don't Need It's revealing your strength-

- ➢ **you've made Still Standing Still Growing.**

You're not behind you're not falling You're Living

…. And that's enough.

Start showing up for this version you Not the perfect one Not the one that has it all figured out but the one who's trying because one day. You'll look back and realize that the version of you who felt Lost was actually the version that was quietly becoming found.

**"Stop waiting for Next thing**

**Stop Running from your present**

**Starting owning it"**

Because Now is all you ever really have. And once you Start Valuing it everything to change

# DAY 3

## "DON'T WAIT FOR SOMEONE TO LEAVE"

## "JUST TO REALIZE HOW RARE REAL CONNECTION IS"

# This chapter is for you

For the one who's doing their Best, even when it's Not Noticed For the one who's healing From things they Never Talk about. For the one who want to give up. But still gets op anyway

For the one who keeps choosing people, who don't choose them back and is finally ready to choose. Themselves.

Not when you graduate. Not when you're Successful. Not when you're fixed.

**NOW...**

The moment you cry but keep going. The times you invisible but still show up. The pain that shape's you. The Lessons that hurts you. The Love you give that.

Sometimes goes unreturned. That is real. That is growth

And Someday, the Same "Now" that feels heavy will become the story that makes you strong.

There will come a day when you'll smile at your Past self-The broken unsure tired version of you and say

> ➤ **Thank you for not Giving up**

You'll realize that everything you hated about Now was actually shaping everything you'll love about your future The tears the pressure, the fake people, the late-Night breakdowns - All of its pushing you closer to the real you

So slow down, stop trying to escape the present moment.

**Look around Feel everything**

**let go of what's fake**

**Hold on to what's real.**

**And trust that you're not Lost -**

**You're just in the part of the story that isn't finished yet!**

So trust the peace of becoming Let Success be Slow and the friendship be few but real. Forgive yourself for yesterday. Release your grip on tomorrow. And meet yourself here, in the only place you have ever truly Lived Now is not perfect, but it is honest lean into its Imperfection with your whole, beating unfiltered heart. And watch how life at last begins.

**~at lowest time, you realize alottt…**

# Chapter 4

# Value Before they leave!

**Focusing** on realizing the value of people before key leave-Written in an emotional, reflective style to deeply connects with readers.

We don't always see the value of someone when theyre still around

We get used to their presence - the messages they send when we're quiet. The way they remember the little things, the comfort of knowing they're just a call away, we assume they'll always be there. So we reply date, cancel Plans take their love for granted thinking.

**THEY "LL UNDERSTAND**

And Sometimes they do

until they don't.

One day the messages stop. The calls you once the energy changes ignored never come again. And suddenly you're Scrolling through old chats, re-reading the conversations where they gave you pieces of their heart, and you realize. They were showing up for you long before you even Noticed.

The truth is, we rarely recognize a person's worth when they're beside us. We only realize it when the Beat Next to us is empty- when the listener.

> ➢ "Let's catch up"

We live as if people are permanent that but even the best ones have a limit even the most loyal hearts grow tried of being taken for gradated.

So Look around you now

That friend who keeps checking in

The family member who waits for you at dinner

The one person who Notices when you're voice Sounds different

Tell them you're grate full

Be present when they Speak.

choose them back - Before life teaches you have much it hurts to miss Someone who was once right in front of you.

**Valve them Now**

**Love them Now**

**Before used to becomes**

**all you have left.**

**'SHE WAS ALWAYS THERE'**

He never really noticed how much she did.

She was the kind of friend who remembered his Important dates even when he forgot her owns she'd send long messages on his bad days check in quietly.

Celebrate him loudly. Whenever he had a problem. She listened without judgments. She made Space for him every time.

## Still I Stayed

But He? He showed up when it was Convenient.

Replied...

when he had time. Forgot promises missed Calls, changed plans last minute. He always assumed she'd understand.

And she did. For a while until one day she stopped texting first. She stopped reminding him of the bond they once had. She stopped being there.

At first he didn't Notice. Life was busy. College, work distractions. New friends. But Slowly. He began to feel the Silence. There was No messages on his birthday. No comforting reply when he had a breakdown Just.... quiet. That's when it hit him –how present she had been ;and how absent he had in return...

He typed. Hey.... I miss you But she didn't reply.

Maybe she had already moved on (or) may be she just didn't have the energy anymore to hold into something so One-sided.

He sat there, phone in hand, regret in his chest.

Because the thing about real people is –

**They won't force you to value them. "**

They'll give you Love quietly. And when they're gone they leave even quieter And by the time you realize what they meant. it's too late.

**People don't always leave with anger**

- Sometimes, they leave with silence.

**"Seen but Never felt**

They talked every day memes, Reels good meaning and Late-Night typing bubbles To anyone watching. They Looked close, But in reality there was distance - The kind that Grows in silence between two people" who forgot how to speak their truth.

She shared her life online-filtered Smiles song lyrics in captions, carefully created stories. And he never reacted he just sent. A heart. A laugh. A fire Emojis

But when she posted Something sad, a song about feeling lost (or) went quiet for day's.... he never asked why. He just kept double-tapping. like everything is okay.

Because in this Generation Love is fast and fragile. Friendships is measured in replies.

And presence is often confused with attention.

She craved connection - Not just someone to see her but someone to feel her. To notice the tremble in her Voice. To Ask twice when she Said I'm fine

But he was busy-with life with trends with everything but her Soul.

**One day she deleted the chats.**

**Not out of anger**

**Out of acceptance**

She realized she was trying to build real bond in a world that teaches us to stay casual.

That maybe she was too deep far Someone who only know how to swim on the surface.... He Noticed she was gone when her stories disappeared He opened their chats and saw Nothing.

**Just Silence.**

- ➢ He typed "Hey!
- ➢ No Reply.

**How the Generation works!**

**- We Notice people only after they've stopped Showing up.**

# Day 4

THINGS WE LOVE ARE LIKE THE LEAVES OF THE TREE

THEY CAN FALL ANY-MOMENT WITH A GUST OF WIND

# Chapter 5

# Importance of Being Present

Right Now. Some of us are sitting in classrooms staring at Books; we can't focus on pretending to be fine while quietly breaking inside. Some of us are smiling in front of friends who feels more like Strangers.

Some of us Scroll for hour. Hoping the Screen fills something the real world can't Some of US feel surrounded by people-and still feel completely alone

**This is the reality of Now**

**'Struggling in Silence'.**

College doesn't just give degree It Silently breaks People too.

You wake up tired. You push yourself through assignment, expectations. And comparisons. You smile with your friends, while your minds racer with fears you never Say out loud. You carry pressure - from your family, your personals&.

Yourself....

> ➤ But Pain isn't a competition.

Struggle isn't less real just because you hide it well. And Silence doesn't mean Strength.

What Now Teache you.

Now teaches you who's really there for you!

Not everyone who walk& with you is walking for you! Learn to read energy Not words!

Now teaches to choose yourself....

Not in a selfish way -In a Healing way, you don't own anyone the version of you that's breaking just to keep them comfortable.

– STAYING WHOLE"

"You don't have to break just because they did. You don't have to shrink to be loved louder.

Some people only notice your worth once they can't reach it. So stay whole—even if they call you distant.

Stay kind—even if they weren't.

You owe yourself the love you gave away too freely. Breathe. Heal. Repeat. "

~NAGAMALLI-MANASVI

# Day 5

**NOT EVERYONE YOU LOSS IS A LOSS.**

**SOME EXITS ARE DISGUISED BLESSINGS**

# Chapter 6

# The Art of Laziness

**The Art of Doing Nothing - and Still healing.**

In a world where everyone is running. I Chose to sit down. It wasn't because I was tried - It was because I'm done. Done chasing timelines. Done competing. with people Who weren't even paying attention to me. Done pretending I was okay when all I really wanted to boas a Break

There's something powerfull about Stopping.

Not quitting - Stopping.

Stopping to breathe

Stopping to Notice what your body is Saying.

Stopping to hear your own heart again.

For years, I thought rest was laziness that if I wasn't productive I was falling behind That If I took a break. Someone else would take my place.

> ➢ I woke up! But I stayed in Bed"

There was a day when I woke up early. alarms ringing. Message's waiting-But I didn't get up. I just stayed in Bed. Not because I was Left in me. Lazy But because I had Nothing left in me

The burnout wasn't Loud. It was silent. Like breathing through a fog Like Smiling when you're empty

My mind told me. Get up. You're wasting time But my Soul whispered: stay. You've earned rest.

So. for the first time. I listened to the quieter voice.

I stayed in bed. I cried a little. I started at the crying I did nothing-and Somehow. Everything changed.

I didn't Need advice. I didn't Need motivation I Needed Space

- ➢ Space to exist without expectation....
- ➢ Space to feel without guilt...

**The day, I learned: rest is Not the Opposite of growth - It's the part...**

- ➢ **We always Skip**

# Day 6

## 'WHATEVER YOU DO, NEVER RUN BACK TO WHAT BROKE YOUU"

# Chapter 7

# The Silent Distance

**Family in the Present Generation.**

The Beginning We All know.

We were raised in homes filled with noise.

-Not always the good kind.

There was always a TV playing in the background a Parent on the Phone, Siblings yelling. utensils clattering in the Kitchen. We didn't realize then that Noise and Connection are Not the same. We lived Together. But Sometimes it felt like we didn't Known each other.

Our fathers were tired our mothers often quiet. We thought Silence meant peace

- But Now we known Silence often hidden pain

**It speaks directly to heart….**

One day She sat in her room. The lights dim. her phone in her hand - Not texting, Not Scrolling just holding it waiting. Hoping. The last conversation with her mother had ended in silence - Not the calm kind, but the heavy kind. The kind that lingers like a storm that Never fully Passes. Her Dad had walked past her that morning Looked at her for a Second wanted to say Some- thing

**-but didn't**

Because somewhere along the years, that closeness they once had had faded into cold routine.

She wanted to Ask to go movie 1 if he was okay too But she didn't. They used to laugh together. Now they barely looked at each other at dinner. At School, She used to tell her friends everything. -how her mom made her dose in a heart shape when she was Sad. How her dad waited outside her class with her water bottle.

Now all she said was "I'm good even when she wasn't She didn't hat her parents. She Still Loved them. But dove felt harder to show now. They still asked her about marks, about food about college But Never ask !

**How's your heart?**

**Are you Sleeping okay?**

**what are you afarid these days?**

End of these....

➢ They didn't stop loving you, they just didn't know how to show it in the way you needed. Teach them gently. Love is language we Can always relearn.

# DAY 7

"THE WRONG PEOPLE TEACH YOU THE RIGHT LESSONS.

' LET THEM GO, BUT THANK THEM SILENTLY"

## Chapter 8

# Left Behide

**For the parents who gave everything - And Now sit in silence.**

One day. Time was early morning 6:00 clock. In city full of traffic Sound. Ravi stood at the gate, watching the cab drive away....

His Son was finally learning for the us for the Big Job the bigger dreams RAVI didn't cry. He just waved. Smiled, and whispered to himself...

**"FLY High. Beta"**

Inside Lakshmi had already started folding the blankets from their son's room. The room looked exactly the same except now it felt colder. They had spent 24 years raising him. Skipping New Clothes so he could wear the best uniform.... Saying no to Vacations so he could go to tuitions...Eating less so he could eat more. Smiling through their storms - because his future was their only dream. And Now the house had Only echoes. In the frist few months. Their Son

would call every Sunday video calls, long talk's photos of food and New places. His eyes Sparkled and their too.... But as the months turned into years. the calls become shorter too...Then rarer Then just messages Then...silence, masked as Busy...

They Never complained They just waited Because that's what Love does - it waits, even when it hurts    One day evening Lakshmi, his mother placed

two plates on the table. She paused. Shall I keep one more    Just in case he Calls

and says he's coming?

She asked a hopeful smile on her face....

Ravi, his father looked at her, Swallowed the Jump in his throat and nodded.

Keep it maybe tomorrow"

.... years passed. The walls grew older, the paint chipped the laughter faded

They'd hear of their Son's promotions, vacations his new house But they hadn't seen him in five years. And on one ordinary afternoon his father Ravi Sat by the window and Softly side. We didn't raise him so he'd be rich we raised him so we wouldn't be strangers...lakshmi; his mother didn't reply.... She just held his hands - like she always did when words felt useless...

After along gap......

One day, the Son returned - unexpectedly. He walked in, older, confident, dressed in success - but something inside him cracked when he saw the house. It looked the Same.... But lifeless He found his father asleep on the armchair. He found his mother quietly praying in pooja Room.

He touched their feet - for the first time in years and teare Golled down without warning...I got everything, I wanted but I the ones who gave me everything...

Finally thing....

**Not every child returns**

**Not every parent complains**

**But somewhere in every home, there's chair kept for a child who might never come back.**

**And in every parent's heart, there's**

The most expensive Gift your parents ever gave you.... was their youth

> ➢ Don't repay it with absence…

# Day 8

## THE WAY THEY LEAVE

## TELLS YOU EVERYTHING...

# Chapter 9

# The Strong One

**Behind her Smile lived a Story…. No one asked about**

Her Name was Aadhya. The girl who everyone Loved being around. The One who made jokes at the Home dinner table who picked up everyone's broken pieces and fixed them like her own…The one who never said" No" Never asked for help Never cried in front of anyone. "But No one ever stopped to Ask who holds Aadhya when she breaks? She lost her father when she was 17 suddenly without warning one minute he was there, and the next…. a photo on the wall. Her mother fell into Silence. Her younger brother Stopped eating The relatives whispered.

She has to be strong now

**So Aadhya become Strong**

Not because she wanted ton    But because she had No choice

She learned how to fill bank forms, Run to electricity, office, negotiate with plumber Pay College fees, and bring home groceries - All while pretending everything, was okay.

She would cry in the bathroom quietly. And come out Smiling.

Because her mother needed to see her strong because her brother needed to believe everything was Still Safe. She gave up her dreams of studying abroad stayed back worked a Small Job made it big. Over time - Step by Step, Silently.

**Never complained.**

when she got married everyone Said "She's lucky Her husband is understanding But No one knew how she swallowed insults from in-laws with a Smile just to keep peace…

How she hide her tears during arguments and made Sure her husband Never felt less Supported.

Yet No one cried here.

**Years passed.**

She bought a house

Took care of her mother

Paid for her bother's wedding Helped her husband business grow.

Had a child of her own and raised him with both softness and strength.

**One Rainy evening -**

She sat on the balcony her child asleep her husband out of town her von other Watching TV. And for the first time in years, she let herself cry...

- ➢ Not because she was sad.
- ➢ But because she had survived

Because she realized No one had ever asked her "Aadhya.... what ABOUT YOU?

- ➢ Because some warriors don't wed armos They wear Smiles....

# DAY 9

### "WHEN THEY DON'T STAY"

"Some people are just chapters, not the whole book. They enter, leave fingerprints on your soul,

then walk away without turning back. You'll replay it, trying to make sense.

But don't waste your peace on questions with no answers.

You were never the problem—you were the lesson. "

~MANASVII

# Chapter 10

# Life is Like a Cinema

**Some plays the hero, Some play the villain. But the real fighters?**

Her Name was "Mira". And every day she Played all the roles in her story - the lead, the support the director, and the background crew. she left her hometown at 19. with one bag I three thousand rupees and a heart full of fore. Everyone Said she's too emotional

She'll come back in month" But Mira never turned back.

**Act 1: Struggles & Dreams**

She worked at a call centre Then at a bakery…Then as a content writer She changed roles more than an actor on a movie Set-not because she was confused, but because Survival didn't give her the luxury of choice Some Nights, she cried into hear pillow after being shouted at by her boss. Some days. She smiled through interviews after Skipping lunch to save auto fare. But one thing never changed – she believed one day her, life would be on watching….

**Act 2: love & lesson;**

She fell in love Once hard Deep The kind of love where ever silence feels full

But like most movies, this one had o twist He said she was too focused on herself He Left because you're independent". Mira I don't feel needed

She didn't beg She didn't seam

She Just closed the chapter, poured herself a drink and whispered you were a side role, not the climax.

**Becoming Her own hero.**

Years passed…She got better Not. Just at work, but at being alone without feeling lonely She traveled solo. Paid her EMIS, Read books, Sent money home missed Peoples who never Checked in Forgave those who left without warning She built her world one brick at a time. And when it rained. She held her umbrella alone - still Smiling. People clapped when she got her promotion. But they didn't see the nights she stayed up teaching herself everything YouTube had to offer.

They Said you're So lucky. She Smiled Because they Saw the cinema - not be hide the Scene,

- ➤ But Now She had peace

**Not every film Needs a hero to Save the day**

**Some Stories shine because the Lead Saved herself.**

# Chapter 11

# People Leaving Without Warning

Some people promise forever, and still desire they were never meant to stay.

**No Fights, No drama. No hints…**

Just One unread messages. One Cold reply.

And Then - Nothing.

Ram, had been her best friend for five years Form late-Night Voice calls to helping each others. through Breakups. He was her safe place. The kind of friends who know what her silence meant. Who'd order her favorite food when she was sad? Who never forgot her birthday even when No one else remembered. She used to think No matter what happens in life

> ➢ I have Ram….

**But people don't always leave after storms**

**Sometimes they just fade.**

One day…. It started with flower replies. Then missed calls. Then unread text. Then, came the moment she knew he already gone he Just didn't so Goodbye. She waited for days Checked his last seen. Typed long paragraphs and erased them Cried herself to sleep while his playlist kept Playing in the background. She kept thinking **Did I do something worng"?**But Silence Never Answers She Never got closure to anyone. No apology. not even a Take care.

**It broke her.**

Not Just the absence but the way he made it look so easy to leave….

As if the memories meant Nothing…As if she was just a chapter he finished reading.

**But here's the cruel part-**

She still missed him. Even after everything. She still wished he'd come back and explain Sometimes it Just gives us endings

*After a gap….*

It Took months to healing of learning to stop checking his profile. of deleting their old chats. Of realizing that you can miss someone and Still move on.

**Six months Later.**

She was walking down the same road. This time with a friend who never left her on road…She laughed freely. Lived softly. And when

Someone mentioned his name she didn't flinch. Because now she understood.

He was a Season, not a forever And Just because someone leaves. doesn't mean your Story ends.

They're just a chapter

Not the book...

*LIVE in the MOMENT*

Sometimes, life feels like a whirlwind, rushing us from one task to the next. In the chaos, it's easy to forget to be present, to feel the warmth of the sun on your skin, or to savor that first sip of coffee in the morning. Living in the moment isn't about forcing yourself to be happy all the time; it's about finding peace with where you are, right now. Start by slowing down, just a little. Notice the small details the way the leaves rustle in the wind, the sound of laughter from a nearby conversation, or the rhythm of your own breath.

These are the moments that often go unnoticed but hold the power to ground you. When your mind starts racing with worries about the future or regrets from the past, gently bring it back to the present. It's okay if it wanders; that's just what minds do. What matters is your choice to come back, over and over again. When you're feeling overwhelmed or stuck in your head, reconnect with your senses. Feel the texture of the ground beneath your feet, or let your fingertips brush against something soft and comforting.

Engaging with your senses pulls you back into your body, reminding you that you are here, in this moment. And don't judge yourself if being present feels hard -it's not something you need to master. Some days, you might find it easier to notice the little things; on others, you might feel lost in thought.

That's okay.

# Chapter 12

# The Becominggg…

Aisha used to think a girl…Perfect hair, clean smoothies A-Schedule that Screamed pinterest perfection But she wasn't ' her she was the forgotten one Over slept. Late to class cried over boys who forget. Her name the Next day. She hit rock bottom the Night she overheard her mother Say…She has No direction…. maybe not everyone is meant to shine.

Aisha locked herself in her room and cried herself to sleep. That Night changed herself to sleep. Not because She magically found motivation -but because decided Not being okay was her start…

She stopped trying to be the perfect girl. Instead, she becomes present…She Started showing up for herself Drinking water, writing thoughts. Saying No.

Repeating affirmations like lifelines.

**I don't want to be her I won't to be me healed!**

Three years later…She's the one girl who stands for Life advice Not because she's flawless

But because she Survived her own doubt -and kept Going.

**The girl isn't about looks. It's about mindset It's about showing up for the version of you that thought She'd never make it**

# Day 10

IF YOUR ABSENCE DOESN'T AFFECT THEM

THEN...YOUR PRESENCE NEVER MATTERED...

# Chapter 13

# Literally show me a healthy person'

She was twenty-four Her name was SUMA…She had a degree, a Job, an apartment that Smelled like Lavender candles, and a list of coping mechanisms Saved in her. Notes on the outside - She was okay. Not amazing not broken just…. Okay And in this Generation "okay is Sometimes the best you can be She Scrolled past motivational quotes gym selfies, Mental health checklists and people drinking green Juice in Bali Everyone seemed to be chasing something. Healing hustle high vibrations. And yet No one seemed in peace

**One day she googled:-**

How to stop thinking so much?

why do I feel lonely around, people I love? "Am I healing (as) Just avoiding.

But Google doesn't have answer for hearty. That are quietly breaking. Quick

Suma, had, Survived a father who never said…I'm proud of you a mother who loved her but didn't…1 know how to show it and a childhood where he told to be strong before she even learned how to cry…She had been the therapist friend The good daughter The understanding girlfriend.

She had held space for everyone until there was no space left inside her…Then came the night…Alone in her room her chest aching without reason. She whispered out loud to herself…

I Don't know even what health means anymore…

**Not physically**

**Not mentally**

**Not emotional**

And that Night She made a decision

**Not to be perfect**

**No to be cured**

**But to be honest.**

Some months later Someone messaged her…You seems like you have it all figured out…Like you're really healthy she smiled at her screen. No one in fully healthy But some of us are brave enough to stop pretending.

# Day 11

"PIECES OF ME"

"I GAVE AWAY PIECES OF MYSELF HOPING SOMEONE WOULD BUILD A HOME WITH THEM. BUT NOW I'M BUILDING ONE FOR ME—WITH EVERY PIECE I TAKE BACK"

# The psychology of being that girl

Chapter 14

# The Girl Who Gave Everything....

**~saved with heart**

In a town framed by quit hills and bustling...hearts, Lived a girl her name was "Manu" She wasn't known for her wealth (or) power, but for the way her heart beat outside the chest unprotected, wide open ready to serve to give and to Love To her kindness. Wasn't a gesture. It was a way of living.

She' did stay up late to help her friend prepare for exams, knowing she had her own struggles, one day she is coming from office, she saw one old woman, She gave her umbrella to an old woman in the Rain and, she walked home Soaked She donated her first Salary to an orphanage home instead of buying the phone she longed for. Manu believed in goodness in doing what was right even if no one was watching especially then.

But the world did watch - and misunderstood.

Manu best friend-named as Akshitha. she is the one who stands every time for Manu...she loves, supports her in every way as good...one day evening she did call to Manu started crying to come near me. Manu came.... she sat down in front of her crying over a problems of she. Manu stayed the whole night missing her work. The Next morning Later, She overheard, Akshitha mocking her with others calling her desperate for attention Manu Swallowed the hurt maybe Akshitha was Just upset she thought-....

Manu's world began to crack.

She still helped a neighbor's, sick mother. cooked for colleague after surgery, and sent money to a cousin who promised to return it soon. No one returned her calls after they got what they wanted No one asked how she was

The final blow came when her our family. began to whisper that she was too involved in Others' lives" and that maybe she should focus On herself. The people she broke herself for now broke her spirit.

One day evening. She sat alone on a park bench tears, silently tracing paths down on her cheeks. Not because of the betrayals but because she still wished well for every person who hurt her....

That Night Something inside manu shifted

-Not her kindness but her boundaries......

She didn't stop being good person she just Stopped offering herself to those who treated her goodness as Weakness. She started journaling meditating, and focusing her goals. she started treating the peoples as like they behave with herself she Surrounded herself with silence with books and eventually with a few rare Souls who gave as much as they took....

After a Some year.........Years passed!

The girl who gave everything still lived-Just of a little differntly, she smiled more, cried less, and kept her heat safe inside her chest where it belonged she built a life filled with peace family well-wishers Not people who drained her....!

And when someone asked why she was so careful Now,

- ➢ **She Smiled,**
- ➢ **She Replied**

Because I learned the hard way-love, Support and kindness are beautiful things but in this generation it wont work...But only when Shared with those who understand their value.

Manu. No longer, chased people Begged for Loyalty ) broke herself to keep others whole. She walked away from anyone who saw her Light and still chase darkness

She wasn't bitter. Just wiser and that wisdom-It Saved her. But Life, as it does, brought Manu full circle

One afternoon at a library she saw girl Crying silently in a corner, clutching a book as if it were a lifeline. Manu didn't ask questions she simply walked over. Sat beside her a and Said, you're not alone. The girl I Looked up and whispered How did you know I needed someone today! Manu Smiled-Because, I'm once like you

She didn't offer Solution she offered presence Not because, she wanted to fix Someone but because she had finally learned how to be there without Losing herself...

Manu completely changed for herself because now a days every one play game with emotions, feelings, peoples

# Final Note

That day, Manu realized her softness was never the problem. It was her lack of boundaries that caused the pain. Now, with love guarded by wisdom, she helped again — only this time, with balance. She started writing a book. Her words resonated with thousands. She wasn't just healing — she was helping others to heal. Not by saving them, but by inspiring them to save themselves. She became a speaker, a mentor, and eventually an author. Her book, titled STILL I STAYED, became a BEST MOTIVATOR for people who felt too much and received too little.

The girl who once cried silently in a park now stand before hundreds of peoples, sharing her story — not as a victim, but as a survivor. And every time someone said, "Your story sounds like mine, " MANU know she had found her purpose.

**She still gives. But now, she gives wisely.**

A year after her book's release, MANU was invited to a university to speak about emotional strength. Among the crowd, she saw familiar faces — akshitha, her old friend, and even, the boy who once broke her heart.

## Final Note

Akshitha, approached her after the session, not with arrogance but humility. "I didn't understand you back then. I mocked you because I envied how deeply you loved. I'm sorry. "

The boy followed. "I thought kindness was weakness. But you were the strongest person I ever know. I'm not here for forgiveness. Just gratitude. "

Manu looked at them both, her heart calm.

"Life always brings back the lessons we leave incomplete, " she said. "I've forgiven you already, but I've outgrown the space where I needed your apology. "

She walked away with grace, her spirit lighter.

The girl who gave everything had become a woman who gave only what was deserved. Not from bitterness, but from self-respect.

Next day Manu called to akshitha to come for dinner…after they both meet they were started, and restart the friendship again as more than past,,, they are together in anywhere. the pure souls connects again from god support…

And in that, she found the peace she had always longed for.

You can give everything and still Not be enough for people You who don't know the value how to Valve

## Final Note

Don't let them define your worth keep your Softness But "protect it with fire...

# The Ones Who Stayed When No One Else Did!

**(A true story for those who still believe in family love)**

In a world where most girls were fighting to be understood, raji, was blessed with something rare — parents who understood her without her having to say a word.

She wasn't the brightest student in class. Not the prettiest girl in the group. Not the loudest voice in the room. But she had dreams — big, quiet dreams. And every time the world laughed at them, her parents stood silently behind her, holding her up…

When rajii, failed her first board exam, she didn't have to lie or hide. Her father walked into her room, sat beside her, and said, "Marks don't decide your life.

We'll try again. " While others were scolding and comparing, her mother made her favorite food that night. "Let her rest, " she told the world. "She's already tired of herself. "

And that's what love felt like — not loud, not boastful — but present.

In college, raji lost herself. She gave too much to fake friendships, to a boy who used her kind heart and left, to people who drained her spirit. Every time she came home, she smiled like nothing was wrong. But mothers know. Fathers see. One night, she broke down.

"I'm tired, " she said, crying on the floor. "I'm tired of loving people who don't care, of trying hard and failing, of being told I'm not enough. "

Her dad didn't interrupt. He just sat beside her and let her cry. Her mom brought her warm tea and said, "You don't need to be enough for them. You're already everything to us. " That night, raji realized — in a world full of temporary people, her parents were permanent.

When she told them she didn't want to follow the traditional job path and wanted to explore writing, they didn't shout. Her dad only asked, "Do you believe in yourself?" and her mom added, "Then we believe in you too. "

They helped her buy her first laptop. They shared her writings with family, proudly. They defended her when people mocked her "unstable future. " While the world kept asking, "What will she become?" her parents were proud of whom she already was.

Now, years later, when raji is finally publishing her book — this very book — she writes this chapter first.

Because in every story of heartbreak, healing, friendship, and finding herself — there were always two people in the background, silently rooting for her: her parents.

**They never needed to be perfect. They just needed to be there.**

And they were!

In a generation where most are trying to escape home, rajii found home in them.

**Be the One Who Stays" — A Story for the 2K Generation**

This story isn't from a fairytale. It's from now—from the world of Instagram reels, fake "check-up" texts, streaks over substance, and people who preach loyalty but vanish the second you're no longer useful.

It's a story every 2000s kid needs to hear.

# Chapter 1: Everyone Loves You Until you're Not Useful

Anaya was your average 2k girl. She had 1, 200 followers, got birthday wishes from 300 people on her story, and DMs full of "you're my whole soul" from friends who called her their "day one."

But then came the night when everything changed.

Her mother had a stroke. Suddenly, the loud group chats were silent. The one who used to call every day to talk about boys and gossip just sent a dry "stay strong." Some didn't even say that......

She posted less. She stopped replying to memes. She was grieving— and lonely. Guess how many of those 300 "birthday wishers" checked on her a week later? Three…

Only three

And one of them was uday.

## Chapter 2: Uday Didn't Look Loyal — But He Was

Uday wasn't flashy. No aesthetic stories. No big friend circle. But he noticed things others missed. He saw when Anaya's energy shifted. He didn't just react to her posts — he responded to her pain.

He didn't send a long emotional paragraph to post publicly. He sent a quiet message:

- ➢ "I'm not here for likes.
- ➢ I'm here if you need a safe space. No pressure. Just know you're not alone. "

And when Anaya finally broke down and cried on a random Tuesday night, UDAY was the one who stayed on call for four hours, saying nothing—just breathing with her…

## Chapter 3: We Need to Talk, 2K Kids

If you're reading this and you're part of this generation — the "2k kids" — let's be honest.

--We've created a culture where we treat people like Wi-Fi: only useful when they're giving us something. We normalize fake friendships, make memes out of betrayal, and glorify "cutting people off" over communicating. We say "I'm always here for you, " but panic when someone shows us raw emotion. We crave "vibes, " but we run from responsibility.

It's time to change.

Because someday you'll be Anaya — needing someone. And if you've never been that "someone" for others, you might find yourself surrounded by noise but abandoned in silence...

## Chapter 4: Be the One Who Changes the Pattern

Be like uday

Be the person who doesn't just check up when it's trending. Be the person who listens when it's uncomfortable.

Be the one who stays when everyone else leaves.

You don't need to be rich, famous, or popular to be that person. You just need to care deeply and act consistently. That's what real love, real friendship, and real loyalty look like.

And guess what? It's rare.

But you can be that rare one....

This generation doesn't need more followers. It needs more safe spaces.

It doesn't need more filters. It needs more honesty. It doesn't need more people saying "I got you." It needs more people showing up—when it's dark, messy, and real.

**Dear 2k kid,**

You might feel like the world owes you love.

But remember: the love you want starts with the love you give.

Respect those who stayed with you when they had every reason to leave. And more than anything—be that person for someone else.

Because when the hype fades, when the clout dies, when the party ends…

It's the ones who stayed during the storm who truly matter.

And if you become that kind of person, you will matter more than any follower count ever could.

# "Two Silences, One Heart"

> They say men don't cry. But that's not true.

Arjun was 24 when he lost his mother. It was sudden — a heart attack on a quiet Sunday morning. One moment, she was asking him to come have

breakfast. The next, she was gone. The house, once filled with her laughter and voice, felt like a museum of memories.

His father, Mahesh, was 53 — a simple, silent man. The kind who rarely said "I love you, " but showed it by cutting fruits for his son when he studied late, or fixing the broken tap before anyone noticed. He didn't cry during the rituals.

He just stood there — dry-eyed, still, and stoic. But after everyone left and the house was empty, Arjun saw it — his father sitting on the kitchen floor, holding her mangalsutra, weeping like a child.

They didn't talk much after that. Both hurt, both grieving, but neither knowing how to speak it. Arjun thought his father was cold. Mahesh thought his son had moved on too fast.

Then, a year later, Arjun fell in love with a girl named ramya…. She was everything he wanted — kind, vibrant, and full of life. For a while, it felt like sunshine after a long storm. They talked about marriage, about dreams, about forever.

**But forever didn't last.**

One day, ramya left. No explanation. Just a note

**"You love, but you're scared to open up. I need more. "**

It shattered him.

He came home and broke down — really broke down — in front of his father for the first time. The son who always held it together was now on the floor, weeping, whispering, "Why does everyone I love leave?"

And then something unexpected happened.

Mahesh sat beside him, placed his hand gently on his son's head and said, "You know...after your mother died, I didn't cry because I thought I had to be strong for you. But every night, I screamed silently. I looked at your face and kept everything in. "

Arjun looked up, shocked.

His father continued, "I saw you smile through your pain and thought you didn't need me. So, I stayed quiet. Maybe we both were wrong...thinking silence is strength. " That night, for the first time, they spoke — not like father and son, but like two humans carrying too much grief. They spoke about Mom. About the way she laughed. About the way she used to forget the stove was on. They spoke about ramya. About pain. About how hard it is to be a man who feels deeply in a world that expects him to stay strong always.

That conversation didn't fix everything — but

**it became the start of healing.**

They began walking every morning, cooking together, and even laughing again. They didn't fill the silence with noise — they just made space for honesty.

Because grief doesn't leave you. But love, when shared, makes the burden easier to car

**"In a world that teaches men to stay silent, a father and son found healing in breaking it. "**

www.ingramcontent.com/pod-product-compliance
Lightning Source LLC
LaVergne TN
LVHW091318080426
835510LV00007B/534